This publication has been developed by the U.S.
Department of Labor, Employee Benefits Security
Administration (EBSA), and is available on the Web at
www.dol.gov/ebsa.

For a complete list of EBSA publications,
call the agency's toll free number:
1-866-444-3272

This material will be made available in alternate
format upon request:

Voice phone: 202-693-8664
TTY: 202-501-3911

This booklet constitutes a small entity compliance guide for purposes of the
Small Business Regulatory Enforcement Act of 1996.

AN EMPLOYEE'S GUIDE TO HEALTH BENEFITS UNDER COBRA

The Consolidated Omnibus Budget Reconciliation Act

U.S. Department of Labor
Employee Benefits Security Administration

Revised September 2010

CONTENTS

INTRODUCTION

Health insurance programs help workers and their families take care of their essential medical needs. These programs can be one of the most important benefits provided by an employer.

There was a time when employer-provided group health coverage was at risk if an employee was fired, changed jobs, or got divorced. That substantially changed in 1986 with the passage of the health benefit provisions in the Consolidated Omnibus Budget Reconciliation Act (COBRA). Now, many employees and their families who would lose group health coverage because of serious life events are able to continue their coverage under the employer's group health plan, at least for limited periods of time.

This booklet explains your rights under COBRA to a temporary extension of employer-provided group health coverage, called COBRA continuation coverage.

This booklet is designed to:

- Provide a general explanation of your COBRA rights and responsibilities;
- Outline the COBRA rules that group health plans must follow;
- Highlight your rights to benefits while you are receiving COBRA continuation coverage.

WHAT IS COBRA CONTINUATION COVERAGE?

The Consolidated Omnibus Budget Reconciliation Act (**COBRA**) requires most group health plans to provide a temporary continuation of group health coverage that otherwise might be terminated.

COBRA requires continuation coverage to be offered to covered employees, their spouses, their former spouses, and their dependent children when group health coverage would otherwise be lost due to certain specific events. Those events include the death of a covered employee, termination or reduction in the hours of a covered employee's employment for reasons other than gross misconduct, divorce or legal separation from a covered employee, a covered employee's becoming entitled to Medicare, and a child's loss of dependent status (and therefore coverage) under the plan.

Employers may require individuals who elect continuation coverage to pay the full cost of the coverage, plus a 2 percent administrative charge. The required payment for continuation coverage is often more expensive than the amount that active employees are required to pay for group health coverage, since the employer usually pays part of the cost of employees' coverage and all of that cost can be charged to the individuals receiving continuation coverage. The COBRA payment is ordinarily less expensive, though, than individual health coverage. While COBRA continuation coverage must be offered, it lasts only for a limited period of time. This booklet will discuss all of these provisions in more detail.

COBRA generally applies to all group health plans maintained by private-sector employers (with at least 20 employees) or by state and local governments. The law does not apply, however, to plans sponsored by the Federal government or by churches and certain church-related organizations.

Under COBRA, a group health plan is any arrangement that an employer establishes or maintains to provide employees or their families with medical care, whether it is provided through insurance, by a health maintenance organization, out of the employer's assets on a pay-as-you-go basis, or otherwise. "Medical care" for this purpose includes:

- Inpatient and outpatient hospital care;
- Physician care;
- Surgery and other major medical benefits;
- Prescription drugs;
- Dental and vision care.

Life insurance is not considered "medical care," nor are disability benefits; and COBRA does not cover plans that provide only life insurance or disability benefits.

Group health plans covered by COBRA that are sponsored by private-sector employers generally are governed by ERISA. ERISA does not require employers to establish plans or to provide any particular type or level of benefits, but it does require plans to comply with ERISA's rules. ERISA gives participants and beneficiaries rights that are enforceable in court.

ALTERNATIVES TO COBRA CONTINUATION COVERAGE

If you become entitled to elect COBRA continuation coverage when you otherwise would lose group health coverage under a group health plan, you should consider all options you may have to get other health coverage before you make your decision. One option may be "special enrollment" into other group health coverage.

Under the Health Insurance Portability and Accountability Act (HIPAA), if you or your dependents are losing eligibility for group health coverage, including eligibility for continuation coverage, you may have a right to special enroll (enroll without waiting until the next open season for enrollment) in other group health coverage. For example, an employee losing eligibility for group health coverage may be able to special enroll in a spouse's plan. A dependent losing eligibility for group health coverage may be able to enroll in a different parent's group health plan. To have a special enrollment opportunity, you or your dependent must have had other health coverage when you previously declined coverage in the plan in which you now want to enroll. To special enroll, you or your dependent must request special enrollment within 30 days of the loss of other coverage.

If you or your dependent chooses to elect COBRA continuation coverage instead of special enrollment, you will have another opportunity to request special enrollment once you have exhausted your continuation coverage. In order to exhaust COBRA continuation coverage, you or your dependent must receive the maximum period of continuation coverage available without early termination. You must request special enrollment within 30 days of the loss of continuation coverage.

Another option may be to buy an individual health insurance policy. HIPAA gives individuals who are losing group health coverage and who have at least 18 months of creditable coverage without a break in coverage of 63 days or more the right to buy individual health insurance coverage that does not impose a preexisting condition exclusion period. For this purpose, most health coverage, including COBRA continuation coverage, is creditable coverage. These special rights may not be available to you if you do not elect and receive continuation coverage. For more information on your right to buy individual health insurance coverage, contact your state department of insurance.

In addition, individuals in a family may be eligible for health insurance coverage through various government programs, such as Pre-Existing Condition Insurance Plans and the Children's Health Insurance Program. For more information, visit http://www.healthcare.gov/law/provisions/preexisting/index.html and www.insurekidsnow.gov or contact your state department of insurance.

WHO IS ENTITLED TO CONTINUATION COVERAGE?

There are three basic requirements that must be met in order for you to be entitled to elect COBRA continuation coverage:

- Your group health plan must be **covered** by COBRA;
- A **qualifying event** must occur; and
- You must be a **qualified beneficiary** for that event.

PLAN COVERAGE

COBRA covers group health plans sponsored by an employer (private-sector or state/local government) that employed at least 20 employees on more than 50 percent of its typical business days in the previous calendar year. Both full- and part-time employees are counted to determine whether a plan is subject to COBRA. Each part-time employee counts as a fraction of a full-time employee, with the fraction equal to the number of hours that the part-time employee worked divided by the hours an employee must work to be considered full time.

QUALIFYING EVENTS

"Qualifying events" are events that cause an individual to lose his or her group health coverage. The type of qualifying event determines who the qualified beneficiaries are for that event and the period of time that a plan must offer continuation coverage. COBRA establishes only the minimum requirements for continuation coverage. A plan may always choose to provide longer periods of continuation coverage.

The following are qualifying events for a **covered employee** if they cause the covered employee to lose coverage:

- Termination of the employee's employment for any reason other than "gross misconduct"; or
- Reduction in the number of hours of employment.

The following are qualifying events for the **spouse** and **dependent child** of a covered employee if they cause the spouse or dependent child to lose coverage:

- Termination of the covered employee's employment for any reason other than "gross misconduct";
- Reduction in the hours worked by the covered employee;
- Covered employee becomes entitled to Medicare;
- Divorce or legal separation of the spouse from the covered employee; or
- Death of the covered employee.

In addition to the above, the following is a qualifying event for a **dependent child** of a covered employee if it causes the child to lose coverage:

- Loss of "dependent child" status under the plan rules.

QUALIFIED BENEFICIARIES

A qualified beneficiary is an individual who was covered by a group health plan on the day before a qualifying event occurred that caused him or her to lose coverage. Only certain individuals can become qualified beneficiaries due to a qualifying event, and the type of qualifying event determines who can become a qualified beneficiary when it happens. (See "Qualifying Events" earlier in this booklet.) A qualified beneficiary must be a covered employee, the employee's spouse or former spouse, or the employee's dependent child. In certain cases involving the bankruptcy of the employer sponsoring the plan, a retired employee, the retired employee's spouse (or former spouse), and the retired employee's dependent children may be qualified beneficiaries. In addition, any child born to or placed for adoption with a covered employee during a period of continuation coverage is automatically considered a qualified beneficiary. Agents, independent contractors, and directors who participate in the group health plan may also be qualified beneficiaries.

YOUR COBRA RIGHTS AND RESPONSIBILITIES: NOTICE AND ELECTION PROCEDURES

Under COBRA, group health plans must provide covered employees and their families with certain notices explaining their COBRA rights. They must also have rules for how COBRA continuation coverage is offered, how qualified beneficiaries may elect continuation coverage, and when it can be terminated.

NOTICE PROCEDURES

Summary Plan Description
The COBRA rights provided under the plan must be described in the plan's summary plan description (SPD). The SPD is a written document that gives important information about the plan, including what benefits are available under the plan, the rights of participants and beneficiaries under the plan, and how the plan works. ERISA requires group health plans to give you an SPD within 90 days after you first become a participant in a plan (or within 120 days after the plan is first subject to the reporting and disclosure provisions of ERISA). In addition, if there are material changes to the plan, the plan must give you a summary of material modifications (SMM) not later than 210 days after the end of the plan year in which the changes become effective; if the change is a material reduction in covered services or benefits, the SMM must be furnished not later than 60 days after the reduction is adopted. A participant or beneficiary covered under the plan may request a copy of the SPD and any SMMs (as well as any other plan documents), which must be provided within 30 days of a written request.

COBRA General Notice
Group health plans must give each employee and each spouse who becomes covered under the plan a **general notice** describing COBRA rights. The general notice must be provided within the first 90 days of coverage. Group health plans can satisfy this requirement by giving you the plan's SPD within this time period, as long as it contains the general notice information. The general notice should contain the information that you need to know in order to protect your COBRA rights when you first become covered under the plan, including the

name of the plan and someone you can contact for more information, a general description of the continuation coverage provided under the plan, and an explanation of any notices you must give the plan to protect your COBRA rights.

COBRA Qualifying Event Notices
Before a group health plan must offer continuation coverage, a qualifying event must occur, and the group health plan must be notified of the qualifying event. Who must give notice of the qualifying event depends on the type of qualifying event.

The **employer** must notify the plan if the qualifying event is:

- Termination or reduction in hours of employment of the covered employee;
- Death of the covered employee;
- Covered employee's becoming entitled to Medicare; or
- Bankruptcy of the employer.

The employer has 30 days after the event occurs to provide notice to the plan.

You (the covered employee or one of the qualified beneficiaries) must notify the plan if the qualifying event is:

- Divorce;
- Legal separation; or
- A child's loss of dependent status under the plan.

You should understand your plan's rules for how to provide notice if one of these qualifying events occurs. The plan must have procedures for how to give notice of the qualifying event, and the procedures should be described in both the general notice and the plan's SPD. The plan can set a time limit for providing this notice, but the time limit cannot be shorter than 60 days, starting from the latest of:

(1) the date on which the qualifying event occurs; (2) the date on which you lose (or would lose) coverage under the plan as a result of the qualifying event; or (3) the date on which you are informed, through the furnishing of either the SPD or the COBRA general notice, of the responsibility to notify the plan and the procedures for doing so.

If your plan does not have reasonable procedures for how to give notice of a qualifying event, you can give notice by contacting the person or unit that handles your employer's employee benefits matters. If your plan is a multiemployer plan, notice can also be given to the joint board of trustees, and, if the plan is administered by an insurance company (or the benefits are provided through insurance), notice can be given to the insurance company.

COBRA Election Notice
When the plan receives a notice of a qualifying event, the plan must give the qualified beneficiaries an election notice, which describes their rights to continuation coverage and how to make an election. The notice must be provided to the qualified beneficiaries within 14 days after the plan administrator receives the notice of a qualifying event. The election notice should contain all of the information you will need to understand continuation coverage and make an informed decision whether or not to elect continuation coverage. It should also give you the name of the plan's COBRA administrator and tell you how to get more information.

COBRA Notice of Unavailability of Continuation Coverage
Group health plans may sometimes deny a request for continuation coverage or for an extension of continuation coverage. If you or any member of your family requests continuation coverage and the plan determines that you or your family member is not entitled to the requested continuation coverage for any reason, the plan must give the person who requested it a notice of unavailability of continuation coverage. The notice must be provided within 14 days after the request is received, and the notice must explain the reason for denying the request.

COBRA Notice of Early Termination of Continuation Coverage
Continuation coverage must generally be made available for a
maximum period (18, 29, or 36 months). The group health plan may
terminate continuation coverage earlier, however, for any number
of specific reasons. (See "Duration of Continuation Coverage" later
in this booklet). When a group health plan decides to terminate
continuation coverage early for any of these reasons, the plan must give
the qualified beneficiary a notice of early termination. The notice must
be given as soon as practicable after the decision is made, and it must
describe the date coverage will terminate, the reason for termination,
and any rights the qualified beneficiary may have under the plan or
applicable law to elect alternative group or individual coverage, such as
a right to convert to an individual policy.

Special Rules for Multiemployer Plans
Multiemployer plans are allowed to adopt some special rules for
COBRA notices. First, a multiemployer plan may adopt its own
uniform time limits for the qualifying event notice or the election
notice. A multiemployer plan also may choose not to require employers
to provide qualifying event notices, and instead to have the plan
administrator determine when a qualifying event has occurred.
Any special multiemployer plan rules must be set out in the plan's
documents (and SPD).

ELECTION PROCEDURES

If you become entitled to elect COBRA continuation coverage, you
must be given an election period of at least 60 days (starting on the
later of the date you are furnished the election notice or the date you
would lose coverage) to choose whether or not to elect continuation
coverage.

Each of the qualified beneficiaries for a qualifying event may
independently elect continuation coverage. This means that if both you
and your spouse are entitled to elect continuation coverage, you each
may decide separately whether to do so. The covered employee or the

spouse must be allowed, however, to elect on behalf of any dependent children or on behalf of all of the qualified beneficiaries. A parent or legal guardian may elect on behalf of a minor child.

If you waive continuation coverage during the election period, you must be permitted later to revoke your waiver of coverage and to elect continuation coverage as long as you do so during the election period. Under those circumstances, the plan need only provide continuation coverage beginning on the date you revoke the waiver.

The Trade Adjustment Assistance Act of 2002 amended COBRA to provide certain workers who lose their jobs due to the effects of international trade and who qualify for trade adjustment assistance (TAA) with a *second* opportunity to elect COBRA continuation coverage. For more information about the operation and scope of the second COBRA election opportunity created by the Trade Act, call the HCTC Customer Contact Center at 1-866-628-HCTC (4282) (TDD/TTY: 1-866-626-HCTC (4282)). You may also visit the HCTC Program Web site at www.irs.gov by entering the keyword: "HCTC."

BENEFITS UNDER CONTINUATION COVERAGE

If you elect continuation coverage, the coverage you are given must be identical to the coverage that is currently available under the plan to similarly situated active employees and their families (generally, this is the same coverage that you had immediately before the qualifying event). You will also be entitled, while receiving continuation coverage, to the same benefits, choices, and services that a similarly situated participant or beneficiary is currently receiving under the plan, such as the right during an open enrollment season to choose among available coverage options. You will also be subject to the same rules and limits that would apply to a similarly situated participant or beneficiary, such as co-payment requirements, deductibles, and coverage limits. The plan's rules for filing benefit claims and appealing any claims denials also apply.

Any changes made to the plan's terms that apply to similarly situated active employees and their families will also apply to qualified beneficiaries receiving COBRA continuation coverage. If a child is born to or adopted by a covered employee during a period of continuation coverage, the child is automatically considered to be a qualified beneficiary receiving continuation coverage. You should consult your plan for the rules that apply for adding your child to continuation coverage under those circumstances.

DURATION OF CONTINUATION COVERAGE

Maximum Periods

COBRA requires that continuation coverage extend from the date of the qualifying event for a limited period of time of 18 or 36 months. The length of time for which continuation coverage must be made available (the "maximum period" of continuation coverage) depends on the type of qualifying event that gave rise to the COBRA rights. A plan, however, may provide longer periods of coverage beyond the maximum period required by law.

When the qualifying event is the covered employee's termination of employment or reduction in hours of employment, qualified beneficiaries are entitled to a maximum of **18 months** of continuation coverage.

When the qualifying event is the end of employment or reduction of the employee's hours, and the employee became entitled to Medicare less than 18 months before the qualifying event, COBRA coverage for the employee's spouse and dependents can last until 36 months after the date the employee becomes entitled to Medicare. For example, if a covered employee becomes entitled to Medicare 8 months before the date his/her employment ends (termination of employment is the COBRA qualifying event), COBRA coverage for his/her spouse and children would last 28 months (36 months minus 8 months).

For all other qualifying events, qualified beneficiaries are entitled to a maximum of **36 months** of continuation coverage.[1]

---

[1] Under COBRA, certain retirees and their family members who receive post-retirement health coverage from employers have special COBRA rights in the event that the employer is involved in bankruptcy proceedings begun on or after July 1, 1986. This booklet does not fully describe the COBRA rights of that group.

Early Termination
A group health plan may terminate continuation coverage earlier than the end of the maximum period for any of the following reasons:

- Premiums are not paid in full on a timely basis;
- The employer ceases to maintain any group health plan;
- A qualified beneficiary begins coverage under another group health plan after electing continuation coverage, as long as that plan doesn't impose an exclusion or limitation affecting a preexisting condition of the qualified beneficiary;
- A qualified beneficiary becomes entitled to Medicare benefits after electing continuation coverage; or
- A qualified beneficiary engages in conduct that would justify the plan in terminating coverage of a similarly situated participant or beneficiary not receiving continuation coverage (such as fraud).

If continuation coverage is terminated early, the plan must provide the qualified beneficiary with an early termination notice. (See "Your COBRA Rights and Responsibilities" earlier in this booklet.)

Extension of an 18-month Period of Continuation Coverage
If you are entitled to an 18-month maximum period of continuation coverage, you may become eligible for an extension of the maximum time period in two circumstances. The first is when a qualified beneficiary (either you or a family member) is disabled; the second is when a second qualifying event occurs.

Disability
If any one of the qualified beneficiaries in your family is disabled and meets certain requirements, all of the qualified beneficiaries receiving continuation coverage due to a single qualifying event are entitled to an 11-month extension of the maximum period of continuation coverage (for a total maximum period of **29 months** of continuation coverage). The plan can charge qualified beneficiaries an increased premium, up to 150 percent of the cost of coverage, during the 11-month disability extension.

The requirements are, first, that the disabled qualified beneficiary must be determined by the Social Security Administration (SSA) to be disabled at some time before the 60th day of continuation coverage and, second, that the disability must continue during the rest of the 18-month period of continuation coverage.

The disabled qualified beneficiary or another person on his or her behalf must also notify the plan of the SSA determination. The plan can set a time limit for providing this notice of disability, but the time limit cannot be shorter than 60 days, starting from the latest of: (1) the date on which SSA issues the disability determination; (2) the date on which the qualifying event occurs; (3) the date on which the qualified beneficiary loses (or would lose) coverage under the plan as a result of the qualifying event; or (4) the date on which the qualified beneficiary is informed, through the furnishing of the SPD or the COBRA general notice, of the responsibility to notify the plan and the procedures for doing so.

The right to the disability extension may be terminated if the SSA determines that the disabled qualified beneficiary is no longer disabled. The plan can require qualified beneficiaries receiving the disability extension to notify it if the SSA makes such a determination, although the plan must give the qualified beneficiaries at least 30 days after the SSA determination to do so.

The rules for how to give a disability notice and a notice of no longer being disabled should be described in the plan's SPD (and in the election notice if you are offered an 18-month maximum period of continuation coverage).

Second Qualifying Event
If you are receiving an 18-month maximum period of continuation coverage, you may become entitled to an 18-month extension (giving a total maximum period of **36 months** of continuation coverage) if you experience a second qualifying event that is the death of a covered employee, the divorce or legal separation of a covered employee and

spouse, a covered employee's becoming entitled to Medicare, or a loss of dependent child status under the plan. The second event can be a second qualifying event only if it would have caused you to lose coverage under the plan in the absence of the first qualifying event. If a second qualifying event occurs, you will need to notify the plan.

The rules for how to give notice of a second qualifying event should be described in the plan's SPD (and in the election notice if you are offered an 18-month maximum period of continuation coverage). The plan can set a time limit for providing this notice, but the time limit cannot be shorter than 60 days from the latest of: (1) the date on which the qualifying event occurs; (2) the date on which you lose (or would lose) coverage under the plan as a result of the qualifying event; or (3) the date on which you are informed, through the furnishing of either the SPD or the COBRA general notice, of the responsibility to notify the plan and the procedures for doing so.

Conversion Options
If your group health plan gives participants and beneficiaries whose coverage under the plan terminates the option to convert from group health coverage to an individual policy, the plan must give you the same option when your maximum period of continuation coverage ends. The conversion option must be offered not later than 180 days before your continuation coverage ends. The premium for an individual conversion policy may be more expensive than the premium of a group plan, and the conversion policy may provide a lower level of coverage. You are not entitled to the conversion option, however, if your continuation coverage is terminated before the end of the maximum period for which it was made available.

SUMMARY OF QUALIFYING EVENTS, QUALIFIED BENEFICIARIES, AND MAXIMUM PERIODS OF CONTINUATION COVERAGE

The following chart shows the specific qualifying events, the qualified beneficiaries who are entitled to elect continuation coverage, and the maximum period of continuation coverage that must be offered, based on the type of qualifying event. **Note that an event is a qualifying event only if it would cause the qualified beneficiary to lose coverage under the plan.**

QUALIFYING EVENT	QUALIFIED BENEFICIARIES	MAXIMUM PERIOD OF CONTINUATION COVERAGE
Termination (for reasons other than gross misconduct) or reduction in hours of employment	Employee Spouse Dependent Child	18 months[2]
Employee enrollment in Medicare	Spouse Dependent Child	36 months
Divorce or legal separation	Spouse Dependent Child	36 months
Death of employee	Spouse Dependent Child	36 months
Loss of "dependent child" status under the plan	Dependent Child	36 months

[2] In certain circumstances, qualified beneficiaries entitled to 18 months of continuation coverage may become entitled to a disability extension of an additional 11 months (for a total maximum of 29 months) or an extension of an additional 18 months due to the occurrence of a second qualifying event (for a total maximum of 36 months). (See "Duration of Continuation Coverage" earlier in this booklet.)

PAYING FOR CONTINUATION COVERAGE

Your group health plan can require you to pay for COBRA continuation coverage. The amount charged to qualified beneficiaries cannot exceed 102 percent of the cost to the plan for similarly situated individuals covered under the plan who have not incurred a qualifying event. In determining COBRA premiums, the plan can include the costs paid by employees and the employer, plus an additional 2 percent for administrative costs.

For qualified beneficiaries receiving the 11-month disability extension, the COBRA premium for those additional months may be increased to 150 percent of the plan's total cost of coverage for similarly situated individuals.

COBRA charges to qualified beneficiaries may be increased if the cost to the plan increases but generally must be fixed in advance of each 12-month premium cycle. The plan must allow you to pay the required premiums on a monthly basis if you ask to do so, and the plan may allow you to make payments at other intervals (for example, weekly or quarterly). The election notice should contain all of the information you need to understand the COBRA premiums you will have to pay, when they are due, and the consequences of late payment or nonpayment.

When you elect continuation coverage, you cannot be required to send any payment with your election form. You can be required, however, to make an initial premium payment within 45 days after the date of your COBRA election (that is the date you mail in your election form, if you use first-class mail). Failure to make any payment within that period of time could cause you to lose all COBRA rights. The plan can set premium due dates for successive periods of coverage (after your initial payment), but it must give you the option to make monthly payments, and it must give you a 30-day grace period for payment of any premium.

You should be aware that if you do not pay a premium by the first day of a period of coverage, but pay the premium within the grace period for that period of coverage, the plan has the option to cancel your coverage until payment is received and then reinstate the coverage retroactively back to the beginning of the period of coverage. Failure to make payment in full before the end of a grace period could cause you to lose all COBRA rights.

If the amount of a payment made to the plan is wrong, but is not significantly less than the amount due, the plan is required to notify you of the deficiency and grant a reasonable period (for this purpose, 30 days is considered reasonable) to pay the difference. The plan is not obligated to send monthly premium notices.

HEALTH COVERAGE TAX CREDIT

Certain individuals may be eligible for a Federal income tax credit that can alleviate the financial burden of monthly COBRA premium payments. The Trade Adjustment Assistance Act of 2002 (Trade Act of 2002) created the Health Coverage Tax Credit (HCTC), an advanceable, refundable tax credit for up to 65 percent of the premiums paid for specified types of health insurance coverage (including COBRA continuation coverage). The HCTC is available to certain workers who lose their jobs due to the effects of international trade and who qualify for trade adjustment assistance (TAA), as well as to certain individuals who are receiving pension payments from the Pension Benefit Guaranty Corporation (PBGC). Individuals who are eligible for the HCTC may choose to have the amount of the credit paid on a monthly basis to their health coverage provider as it becomes due, or may claim the tax credit on their income tax returns at the end of the year.

The Trade Adjustment Assistance Health Coverage Improvement Act of 2009, enacted as part of the American Recovery and Reinvestment Act (ARRA), made changes to the HCTC.

The HCTC now pays a greater portion of your health insurance. The tax credit increased to 80 percent of qualified health insurance premiums. Newly-enrolled participants can request to receive a reimbursement or a credit on their HCTC account for qualified payments made while enrolling in the HCTC Program.

The HCTC is available to your family members for a longer period of time beginning in January 2010. Your family may continue receiving the HCTC for up to 24 months after you, the primary eligible individual, enroll in Medicare, get divorced or die.

COBRA coverage also is temporarily extended for HCTC-eligible individuals. TAA-eligible individuals can keep COBRA coverage as long as they continue to be TAA-eligible.

PBGC-eligible individuals may be able to retain their COBRA coverage until death. The PBGC-eligible individual's spouse and dependents can keep the coverage for an additional 24 months beyond that. However, note that this provision, like the rest of the Trade Adjustment Assistance Health Coverage Improvement Act, expires on December 31, 2010. At the time of this printing, these changes to the HCTC - including the new timeframes for extended benefits - are only valid through December 31, 2010.

Electing the COBRA premium reduction under ARRA disqualifies you for the HCTC. If you are eligible for the HCTC, which could be more valuable than the premium reduction, you will have received a notification from the IRS. If you are already receiving the COBRA premium reduction and wish to receive the HCTC, you can switch by opting out of the COBRA premium reduction program prior to registering for the HCTC program. You cannot receive the COBRA premium reduction and the HCTC in the same month.

For more information about the Health Coverage Tax Credit, call the HCTC Customer Contact Center at 1-866-628-HCTC (4282) (TDD/TTY: 1-866-626-HCTC (4282)). You may also visit the HCTC program Web site at www.irs.gov by entering the keyword: "HCTC."

COORDINATION WITH OTHER
FEDERAL BENEFIT LAWS

The Family and Medical Leave Act (FMLA) requires an employer to maintain coverage under any "group health plan" for an employee on FMLA leave under the same conditions coverage would have been provided if the employee had continued working. Group health coverage that is provided under the FMLA during a family or medical leave is **NOT** COBRA continuation coverage, and taking FMLA leave is not a qualifying event under COBRA. A COBRA qualifying event may occur, however, when an employer's obligation to maintain health benefits under FMLA ceases, such as when an employee taking FMLA leave decides not to return to work and notifies an employer of his or her intent not to return to work.

In considering whether to elect continuation coverage, you should take into account that maintaining group health coverage affects your future rights to protections provided under HIPAA. HIPAA limits the length of any preexisting condition exclusion that a group health plan may impose and generally requires any exclusion period to be reduced by an individual's number of days of creditable coverage that occurred without a break in coverage of 63 days or more. For this purpose, most health coverage, including COBRA coverage, is creditable coverage. Electing COBRA may help you avoid a 63-day break in coverage and, therefore, help you eliminate or shorten any future preexisting condition exclusion period that may be applied by a future group health plan, health insurance company, or HMO.

HIPAA also provides special enrollment rights upon the loss of group health plan coverage and rights to buy individual coverage that does not impose a preexisting condition exclusion period as described earlier in this book (See "Alternatives to COBRA Continuation Coverage").

To take advantage of some of HIPAA's protections, individuals must show evidence of prior creditable coverage. The primary way individuals can evidence prior creditable coverage to reduce a preexisting condition exclusion period (or to gain other access to individual health coverage) is with a certificate of creditable coverage. HIPAA requires group health plans, health insurance companies, and

HMOs to furnish a certificate of creditable coverage to an individual upon cessation of coverage. A certificate of creditable coverage must be provided automatically to individuals entitled to elect COBRA continuation coverage no later than when a notice is required to be provided for a qualifying event under COBRA, and to individuals who elected COBRA coverage, either within a reasonable time after learning that the COBRA coverage has ceased or within a reasonable time after the end of the grace period for payment of COBRA premiums. If you do not receive or you lose your certificate and cannot obtain another, you can still show prior coverage using other evidence of prior health coverage (for example, pay stubs, copies of premium payments, or other evidence of health care coverage). For more information about evidencing prior health coverage or your rights under HIPAA, contact EBSA toll free at 1-866-444-3272.

The Affordable Care Act (ACA) provides additional health protections. Except for references to the PCIPs, this publication does not reflect the Affordable Care Act. For more information, visit the Department of Labor's Web page at www.dol.gov/ebsa/healthreform/. Also visit the Department of Health and Human Services (HHS) Web site at www.healthcare.gov.

ROLE OF THE FEDERAL GOVERNMENT

COBRA continuation coverage laws are administered by several agencies. The Departments of Labor and the Treasury have jurisdiction over private-sector group health plans. The Department of Health and Human Services administers the continuation coverage law as it affects public-sector health plans.

The Labor Department's interpretive responsibility for COBRA is limited to the disclosure and notification requirements of COBRA. The Labor Department has issued regulations on the COBRA notice provisions. The Treasury Department has interpretive responsibility to define the required continuation coverage. The Internal Revenue Service, Department of the Treasury, has issued regulations on COBRA provisions relating to eligibility, coverage, and payment. The Departments of Labor and the Treasury share jurisdiction for enforcement of these provisions.

RESOURCES

If you need further information about COBRA, ERISA, or HIPAA, call toll free 1-866-444-3272 to reach the Employee Benefits Security Administration regional office nearest you, or visit the agency's Web site at www.dol.gov/ebsa.

For information about the interaction of COBRA and HIPAA, visit the EBSA Web site, go to "Publications and Reports" and click on *Your Health Plan and HIPAA...Making the Law Work for You.*

The Centers for Medicare and Medicaid Services offer information about COBRA provisions for public-sector employees. You can write them at this address:

Centers for Medicare and Medicaid Services
7500 Security Boulevard
Mail Stop C1-22-06
Baltimore, MD 21244-1850

Federal employees are covered by a Federal law similar to COBRA. Those employees should contact the personnel office serving their agency for more information on temporary extensions of health benefits.

Further information on FMLA is available from the nearest office of the Wage and Hour Division, listed in most telephone directories under U.S. Government, Department of Labor, or visit www.dol.gov/whd.

For questions about TAA, call the HCTC Customer Contact Center at 1-866-628-HCTC (4282) (TDD/TTY: 1-866-626-HCTC (4282)). You may also visit the HCTC Web site at www.irs.gov by entering the keyword "HCTC."

www.ingramcontent.com/pod-product-compliance
Lightning Source LLC
Chambersburg PA
CBHW071346310526
45790CB00018B/1375